By the same editors:
The Missionary Myth (1973)
Grandmas & Grandpas (1975)
To Mum (1976)
To Dad (1976)
Happy Families (1977)

Credits of model photographs:

Cover   The Daily Telegraph Ltd
Page 5   Barnaby's Picture Library
Page 7   John Cowan, Camera Press
Page 9   Claire Schwob
Page 12 Sylvester Jacobs
Page 15 Picturepoint Ltd
Page 16 Pictorial Press Ltd
Page 19 Pictor International Ltd
Page 21 Pictorial Press Ltd
Page 23 G Mangold, Camera Press
Page 25 Sylvester Jacobs
Page 27 Picturepoint Ltd
Page 28 Sylvester Jacobs
Page 31 Pictor International Ltd
Page 32 Sylvester Jacobs
Page 35 Pictor International Ltd
Page 37 Pictorial Press Ltd
Page 39 Pictor International Ltd
Page 40 Barnaby's Picture Library
Page 42 Spectrum Colour Library
Page 47 Pictorial Press Ltd
Page 53 Sylvester Jacobs
Page 56 Claire Schwob
Page 61 Sylvester Jacobs
Page 63 Picturepoint Ltd
Page 67 Claire Schwob
Page 73 Pictorial Press Ltd
Page 75 Pictorial Press Ltd
Page 77 Barnaby's Picture Libary
Page 79 Spectrum Colour Library

Our thanks go to Dee Remington and Diane Hutchinson of Woman Magazine

First Published October 1977.
Second printing December 1977. Copyright © Exley Publications Ltd, 63
Kingsfield Road, Watford, Herts, England, WD1 4PP.
Printed in Great Britain by Chapel River Press, Andover.
Typeset by Beaver ReproGraphics Ltd, 1a Sparrows Herne, Bushey, Herts.
ISBN 0 905521 14 5

Introduction

What is a husband? The answers to that question – pithy, beautiful, downright rude, hilarious, sad, romantic – are everything you might have guessed when real women let fly about their husbands.

In all, over 7,500 people entered a competition held by *Woman* magazine and ourselves, and it was a rewarding experience editing the thousands of replies.

One of the great pleasures of editing the book was comparing the entries to our own marriage, and we are sure this will be compelling for other couples too. You suddenly realise how ridiculous the little battlegrounds of your own marriage are when you see them repeated word for word in someone else's writing. You *laugh* at them in other people's lives.

Lots of letters, of course, came from wives delighted to have a crack at their husbands' expense, and we included a section of these under 'naggers anonymous'. We must have read a hundred letters from aggrieved wives complaining about their husbands' awful feet. And double that number, complaining about their husband's besetting sin of squeezing the toothpaste tube in the wrong place or leaving the top off. Some of the entries were almost books in themselves, forty or fifty pages in length telling the saga of a divorce or break-up. We obviously couldn't include these, but we *have* included several sad entries, and entries from women whose husbands have stood by them through serious hardship or sickness – perhaps these are the most beautiful in the book.

The book contains many sentiments that we would disagree with. But we have tried to be as representative as possible, including entries pro and con Women's Lib.

For obvious reasons we have changed some names, to protect the poor husband. In other cases, where we have quoted a snippet, it would be unfair to attribute this to a wife who had written thousands of adoring words about her otherwise saintly spouse.

The book turned out, in many ways, to be very comforting. Many people obviously build a bond that deepens through the years and some of the warmest entries came from readers who should know – those who've had fifty years and more at the game.

In reading the book you realise that some people's greatest fears – a mastectomy, financial difficulties or simply old age – are as nothing to the ultimate fear of losing the one you love more than anyone else on earth.

What is a husband?

A husband should be felt and not heard.

Yvonne Knight

A husband is a man who when someone tells him he is henpecked, answers, yes, but I am pecked by a good hen.

Gill Karlsen

A husband thinks a male chauvinist pig is the reason we have dearer pork and bacon.

Norma Harris

A husband is someone who lends you his darts — then goes mad if you beat him.

Irene Zuckerman

A husband is the man you let think rules the roost.

Kate Garrett

A husband is the head, but his wife is the neck that turns it.

Pan Grant

Q. How do you spell husband?
A. L.O.V.E.

P T Measor

He likes football, cricket, brown ale, Elizabeth Taylor, Natalie Wood and girls with big boobs; but still claims I'm the one who turns him on.

Ann Greener

A husband is a nuisance I cannot live without!

Molly Porter

A husband is the cheapest form of bed warmer.

P J Wall

He appears to listen to domestic trivia, but when asked about something later says quite bluntly, he's never been told a damn thing.

Esther Cotterell

He is a man who stands by you through all the troubles you wouldn't have had if you had stayed single!

L M Smith

A husband is a bachelor whose luck finally failed.

Janis Young

A husband entangles your heart and happily untangles your head
. . . blooming know-all!

Betty Bolton

A husband never compares your Yorkshire puddings with his
mother's or you with the pin-up on page three.
He says 'I love you' when you're wearing a face-pack; and
remembers your punch-lines for you in public.

Jill Woods

After you have worn a dress for about two years, a husband will
say, 'That's nice, dear, is it new?'

Elizabeth Simms

A husband should not call you his 'old woman'.

Carole Buckler

A good husband is one whose eyes may wander, but whose hands
never do.

T J Jones

He will introduce me to people as his first wife — just to keep me
on my toes!

Rita Law

A husband is a handsome knight on a silver-blue charger with a
matt-vinyl roof.

Dianne Raybould

A husband has to be crafty enough to outwit me, but not silly
enough to think I don't know it.

M C Prickett

He's the guy who makes me say to God every day, 'Thanks for
this guy, God'.

Veronica E Cassidy

He's a *personal* Paul Newman.

Sally V Mantle

*A husband is anticipation,
togetherness without words,
an aggravation
when shopping,
tenderness, the sun,
a body, a look, a touch,
loyalty, ad infinitum.*

Lavinia Allen

Husbands *!?●*_

A husband is the man you commited yourself to for life who indeed becomes a lifetime commitment!

Mary Arvill

A husband is someone who phones you up from the office to ask you the number of his car (parked outside office) and then says 'Thanks, son!'

Patricia Strang

A husband is the man who says, "If you enter that competition on 'What is a Husband?', I'll leave you."

C Tomlinson

In the morning when we wake he turns and whispers to me, "Do you love me? Good. Go make a cuppa tea".

P Williams

A husband leaves tops off things.

Gay Whittaker

He tells you he loves you, pauses a moment and then says he has just burnt a hole in your best table cloth.

Dorothy Lord

A husband is someone who wakes you up when the baby is crying.

R M Walker

A husband is someone who hangs around hungrily when a meal is cooking — then disappears when it's served.

Ina Bourdon

You can let off steam to him and rant and rage, and he'll look up from his newspaper and say 'Did you say something dear?'

Ann Webb

A husband is an escort waiting in blue shirt, pink tie, brown trousers and slippers.

Mary M Breeze

A husband is a man who keeps all other nuisances away, but remains the biggest nuisance.

Jane Radley

When he takes you in his arms he makes you admire your taste in fellows.

Pat Jerred

A husband is . . .

A husband is one who washes up when asked and dries up when told.

Joanna Berry

He's someone from whom 'morning tatty head' is not an insult, but a form of endearment.

Susan Quarrie

A husband is the best thing since sliced bread.

Karen Michelle Kloed

My husband is a wonderful man. The list of his good qualities is extremely long. Unfortunately, I cannot read his writing.

Angela Lansbury

A husband comes home, rushes indoors calling out 'Hallo my precious' and then kisses the cat!

J Rainbow

A husband is everything that a good wife can train him to be.

Patricia Mary Dyson

He's the one you can rely on to rely on you to remember the things he's forgotten.

Lynda Deans

If you are lucky and catch a good one, you can train them to do all sorts of tricks. Every home should have one.

S Clifton

A husband is kind, generous, humorous and loves you. After that you don't need anymore and to pot with his vices!

Melanie Dawson

Even after fifteen years it's like eating soup with a fork, I just can't get enough of him.

Joanne Jones

A husband is someone who sends his wife flowers after *she's* had a bump with the car – yes, he really did!

Guinevere Saunders

A husband is a man that makes me feel like the cat who's got the cream.

Peta Melville-Gardner

He is the gallant who understands how you feel when you first have dentures.

Mary Horton

A husband often tells you that he loves you but never while watching football.

Freda Briant

A husband is someone with a big heart and smelly feet.

Andrea I Leat

A husband is the only person whose socks you'd wash without a shudder.

Linda Cornish

He's the brandy in the Christmas cake,
The seasoning in each dish I bake.
Although I'd sometimes love to clout him,
I can't imagine life without him!

Mary Shilcock

A husband thinks equality for women means that he can get *you* a season ticket for the stand at the football match.

Jennifer Pirie

What is a husband?
He is the man who found me
When I was just a drab, grey mouse.
He took me,
Touched me with his lips,
And I became a tigress.

Christine Kemp

A husband is a man who, when given a wink, comes hither
When given a nod, shuts up
When given a nudge, pays out
When given the chance, goes out.

Sheila Duffill

Domineering devil, a husband – but nice.

Margaret Boyd

*Breadwinninbeerdrinkin
hairthininwaistthicknin
deepsnorinjokeborin
tellywatchinfootballmatchin
eyerovinmelovinHUSBAND.*

Helen H C Bain

**I love every hair
on his balding head.**

Iris Kestell

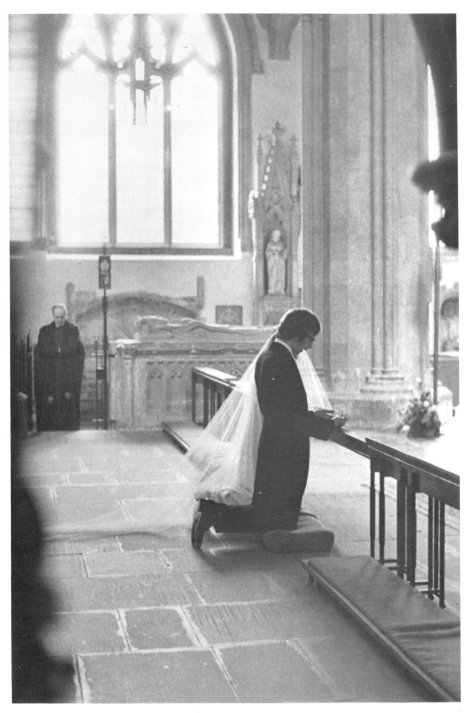

A husband is love

He is the person who fell in love, and when the romantic bubbles burst, continued to love his wife as a person.

Diane Ryder

Happiness is being married to your best friend.

Peggy Welch

My husband is a great big hunk of warmth.

Barbara Kingman

A husband is someone who forgets how important he is.

Ghit-Moy Lee

A husband is someone who has you mad one minute and purring the next.

Irene Taylor

His standing joke 'the best thing you ever did was marry me' is nearer to the truth than he will ever know.

Lyn McGrath

A husband is someone whose total love and dependence is simultaneously terrifying and overwhelmingly wonderful!

Helen Jane Plumbly

You give yourself to him without 'strings' or 'conditions'. He gives himself to you without questions or apologies. A husband needs you and you need him.

J Benn

A husband is a person who lifts you up when you're down, but never lets you down when you're up.

D Langrish

A husband is the man you have chosen to spend the rest of your life with
— to laugh with, to cry with,
to celebrate with,
to mourn with,
but, through all,
to be with, always.

F A Blewitt

13

A husband is someone you cannot hurt without hurting yourself.

D Walkins

As long as I have him and his love and his sometimes odd habits I'd live in a mud hut on the Amazon.

Jenny McVeigh

A husband will get into your hair and under your feet but you can never get him out of your heart.

M E Seamen

A husband softens your sorrows.

Pauline Andrews

A husband is a welcome sight when you step from a train.

Mrs Taylor

A husband is someone to whom you never have to say sorry.

Yvonne L Quirke

A husband is someone who surrounds you with such love and trust that you feel free to explore your potential, knowing he will support you, cherish you in your failures and celebrate your success.

Susan Hardaker

A husband is someone who makes you care — not just for him but for yourself and for everyone in the whole world. He makes you want to share your happiness.

Audrey Susan Squires

We are not rich with money, but love he provides so we must be millionaires.

Liz Todd

My idea of a husband is one who understands me and loves me for the way I am and not for the way he would like me to be.

Sue Salter

He is simply all the good things in life wrapped up in one lovely warm person.

Pauline Jepson

A husband is the man to whom you gave the best years of your life, because he made them the best years of your life.

D C J Fison

There is a particular brand of togetherness with husbands that you can never feel with anyone else.

Hilda J Coumbe

14

If you have a husband like mine, love and keep him for all time.

M S Hardman

To me, a husband is an eternal love affair.

Margare Anne Heap

My husband is humble and when he says, 'Why do you love me? I am so ordinary', it hurts because I can never find the words to tell him he is my whole world.

V M Hales

Marriages are made in Heaven but too often broken on earth.

June Robinson

A husband is half. Half of everything you feel, think, and do. Without him you're only ever half, with him you're a whole that can take on anything.

Jean McKeand

A husband is like a treasure – his value rarely appreciated until it's time to part.

Fiona Lewis

A husband is the man whom you don't realise how much you love and need until you almost lose him to another woman.

Avril Matterson

He's the man in your life to depend on, to have an affair with, a laugh, a cry, to be a father to your kids. I guess a husband is okay.

Carol Clare

When he says 'Good night, love, see you in the morning', you know life would not be worth living if you didn't.

P J Wall

I go cold if I just think of life without him.

Jane Amelia Drew

He is the fella with the huge hands who does a demolition job with the china when helping to dry dishes. Yet those same hands can gently catch a wounded sparrow.

Margaret E Cooper

He is a man who can be gentle, kind, thoughtful — even childlike, but never loses his manliness.

A J Maud

A husband is that someone who made you start thinking about pots and pans and curtains on your second meeting instead of hairdo's, make-up, and clothes, and who has made you automatically think of two rather than one from that time on.

Margaret Klieve

My ideal husband would be an enigma with more variations than Elgar ever dreamed of.

F Wilson

A husband is someone who goes around in the early days of marriage singing 'Everything is beautiful' even though you have no furniture, no money and few prospects!

Patricia Ballantyne

He lights my world with love and laughter. He gives to all my days the warm promise of Spring, and because of him I am ever young. So, darling, for yesterday, today, and all my tomorrows, my love and my thanks.

Catherine Jenkinson

A husband is forever.

J V Palfreyman

He needs my support when he is weak and weary of responsibility. No one knows but me. He is my secret, I am his.

Sue Crabbe

Romantic thoughts

A good husband is a man who treats a wife as if he isn't married to her.

Susan Perkins

He is the one the flowers are always from.

Trisha Goodwin

A husband is someone who brings you the first rose from the garden.

Judith Harris

He is the one you can make 'sweet music' with, in mind, body and soul – the one you love.

Mary Jones

He is someone who takes your heart and keeps it safely next to his for ever and a day.

Lynn Jones

A husband is the man who makes you feel like writing all about him to thousands of people as a way of saying 'I love you' — and I don't mind who knows it.

Margaret Waters

A husband is the best friend you will ever have in your life. He will share your thoughts, your moods, your laughter and your tears. He is your guiding star, someone to live up to and to follow to the ends of the earth. And if that sounds too sentimental, I can't help it, because that's the way I feel about my wonderful husband.

Susan Holmes

A husband would give you the stars if he possibly could.

Julia McKie

A husband is someone with looks of love in his eyes, and his eyes tell you everything from the moment you fall in love, to marriage, to the birth of a child.

Gaynor Ingham

Becoming a father

My husband is the man who dragged me into the car when I'd
finished a day's work, took me into his arms with tears in his eyes
and said, 'Darling, the letter's here, we're going to have a baby'.
He's the man who wanted to wake the whole street the first time
he felt the baby move.
He's the man who when I say 'giving birth worries me' says,
'Don't be frightened, little girl, I'll hold your hand'.
Without him I'm a half.

Linda Thompson

A husband is someone who says you look great even when you
are very pregnant and resembling an Easter egg on legs.

Ann Torrance

A husband heaves you in and out of the bath when you're nine
months pregnant, slaps you on the rump and calls you his 'great
white whale', then tenderly trims the toe-nails you can no longer
reach.

Barbara Mary Prosser

He is the man who suffered all the indigestion, heartburn
and sickness during my pregnancy whilst I bloomed with
health.

Carol McWatt

A husband is someone that asks you for a date, when you're six
months pregnant and pegging out a line of nappies!

Carol Jackson

A husband is a man who claims to be a carefree, selfish, one-of-
the boys type and yet with sweat and tears rolling down his face,
holds your hand while you give birth to his child.

Irene Jamieson

A husband is the man who crosses the maternity ward with a
look in his eyes which says, 'you're the only one who ever had a
baby'.
I've been a widow for over thirty years but I can still remember
that look.

E Storey

*My husband thinks I am
beautiful carrying his
unborn child.*

Margaret Wood

20

Father to your children

A husband is a man who respects you enough to give you his name; who loves you enough to give you his wealth; and who trusts you enough to give you his children.

Irene Sinclair

He is the one that makes you feel like having children — his children.

Diane Young

A husband makes you want to have lots of little children, just like him, running around you.

Janet Dobinson

He is the flesh of your children — children that are born from his and your love.

Dorothy Kennedy

He gently rocks the baby to sleep singing rugby songs.

Lynn Cunningham

He is the mender of broken toys and broken dreams.

Barbara Mary Prosser

A husband is the gentle giant who holds your adopted baby boy in his arms, and says *our son*.

Heather Rooks

A husband is an expert at drying in between tiny toes and fingers.

Lynn Cunningham

He's the guy who cradled his new son in his arms for a whole day between feeds, silent with wonderment.

Veronica E Cassidy

A husband forms a circle of love that gathers in the whole family.

S Manuelpillai

A husband is a pair of arms that work for you, try and move mountains for you, and yet hold your first-born child as if she were porcelain.

Susan Underwood

Love is blind

A husband is someone who calls me 'princess' when I look my worst.

Jennifer Goodwin

When we go to a dinner dance I can see all the lovely elegant ladies and me being short and of plump size (I am Italian) I ask my husband if I am looking nice enough and with his kind and loving eyes he says to me, 'don't worry my darling you are the best lady here' and I just walk by his side very proud and happy and I feel really to be a Queen.
I wish to all the Ladies and future wives to be able to find one marvellous partner in their life.

Novella Gulliver

A husband is a person who remembers your birthday, but not your age.

Carol McGarrity

A husband is someone who forgets your birthday, forgets your anniversary, but also forgets your grey hairs and wrinkles.

Betty Morris

A husband is the great guy who, after thirty-one years of marriage, looks fondly at my twelve stone plus — and sees the slim girl he married.

Winifred Thompson

A husband is someone who kisses your runny eyes when you're full of a cold, and tells you you're lovely.

M Waddington

A husband is someone who comes home from work early to find me in the middle of a secret home beauty treatment, porridge on my face, cold teabags balanced on my eyes, yogurt combed through my hair, and can still give me a hello squeeze — and say 'you're beautiful!'

Maria Parkin

He makes me feel like a 'million dollars' in a room crowded with beautiful girls.

Pauline Rimmer

A husband is someone who tells you you look smashing when you've just woken up in the morning, with makeup smudged all over your face and two slits with bags under for eyes.

Susan Saunders

A husband is someone who can still love you after twenty years of seeing you as no one else does — first thing in the morning!

V A Le Fevre

A husband believes in you when the rest of the world doesn't. He makes you feel 'special' — regardless of looks or age — simply because he invited you to share his world.

Janet Swanton

A husband insists he can't see any grey hairs.

Rosemary Treagust

When your hair needs washing;
When you've got a spot on your chin;
When you have to hold it all in to get it all in;
When you look in the mirror and look away again, quickly;
A husband is someone who says
'Hey — I don't half fancy you'.

Linda E Mackey

The family man

A husband is the man who preferred me above all others to be his wife and the mother of his children.

Ursula Rowlands

A husband is the one who gave me immortality — my children.

Marion Vincent

A husband is a man whose qualities you would like to see come out in your children.

J Edwards

A husband is an athlete of superb prowess, who chases absconding children, taxis and dogs stuck in rabbit holes.

Pauline Davies

A husband is the man your little boy looks like, and your little girl loves best.

Veronica Breedon-Smith

A husband is a loving, mature man until his first son is born. Then he starts his second childhood, playing with train sets, cars, and pretends he's a horse by jumping about with our son on his back and a big grin on his face.

Julie Thomas

He has a very short fuse on his temper and has come home in bad form and after raising a row has got back into the car, driven round the block, and came back home shouting 'Daddy's home', as if it was his first arrival. Then he asks, 'Who was that cross old fellow who was here a minute ago?'
That's just him.

Maureen Blaney

My husband is a wonderful father to my seven children by my first husband. He is the only man in the world who would take on a ready made family and shares our animals, which are two dogs, eleven guinea pigs, one mouse, six gerbils, three rabbits, a hampster, two goldfish and a tortoise.

P A Pritchard

I would have more children, just to see them grow up looking like him.

Lynn Walton

My husband is the type of man I hope my daughter will marry.

Brenda Calvert

My husband is the one and only person in the world who I can rely on to recall the dazzling highbrow conversation I *can* enter into, even though I may be discussing Johnny's runny nose or Laura's tummy-ache.

J Hay

A husband is the beautiful young man with whom I immediately fell in love. I can't resist his beautiful eyes, even when I'm angry. I hoped out children would inherit his eyes, and my hopes were fulfilled.
I would have more children just to see them grow up looking like him.

Lynn Walton

Sharing, building together

A husband is the fellow you fight with — make up with — laugh with and cry with — play with and work with — love with and hurt with — sow with and reap with.

N C Halloway

A husband is someone to love and share all your ups and downs with, while loving the ups and wishing they could last forever, but also coming through the downs together and still being very much in love.

Audrey Lane

Each crisis you share deepens the bond between you so that, eventually, the very strength of your love enables you to give each other the freedom to be yourselves.

Carol Ebden

A husband is someone who you can tell your wildest dreams, and he will not laugh, in fact in his own way he will try and make those dreams come true.

J Brown

My husband is the person on the other end of my personal seesaw.

Vera E J Seaman

Phil is my alter-ego. He is my measuring stick. If he laughs I'm being funny. If he understands I'm communicating and not shouting. He is my father, brother, my best bitching friend, my lover, my critic.
All these things I can live without. Why is he so indispensable? Because I'm his alter-ego, measuring stick, mother, sister, friend, lover, and critic.
I'm needed.

Maria Roberts

He's a man who says 'we' not 'I'.

Helen Anderson

Some say a husband can't be changed. Untrue. Both partners change in an equal marriage, and he's the man who you finally reach the finishing line with, because he's there beside you, not in front of or behind you.

Gillian D S Warner

Mister Teddy Bear

A husband is the only labour-saving device you can cuddle!

Jane Lawrence

A husband is a man called Teddy Bear. He smothers you with warm furry kisses, and calls you Womble.

Joy Roberts

A husband replaces your childhood teddy bear with the added advantage that not only does he grunt but he talks as well.

L Shrapnell

If you have to spend a night away from him, you can't sleep properly, because his arm isn't wrapped around you. He is the person you shared the single bed with (before you could afford a double), and the person who makes a double bed seem like that old single. He tickles you and calles you Wonder Wabbit Woman, cossets you and makes you feel sixteen again when you are actually forty-two.

Joy Roberts

A husband can make you feel safer than all the doors and locks.

June McDermott

29

A sense of security

After a rotten day when nothing has gone right, the sound of your husband's key in the door is like being wrapped in a lovely warm blanket.

Sheila G Reynolds

A husband is the beginner of your whole new life and is there at the end when the children are gone. Still a rock to lean upon.

Dorothy Kennedy

A husband makes you feel special by telling you that no one is going to hurt you while he's around.
He makes you feel unbelievably precious, which is the most wonderful thing one human being can do for another.

Elizabeth Edwards

A husband is a man who makes his partner feel so secure and stable, that she is thus given the courage and love to rear the next generation, and give them the stability to ask questions and not be afraid of the answers.

Wendy Wright

A husband is a wonderful man that can squeeze your hands and comfort you, when you know he is crying inside, as you both sit by your son's bedside after a critical eye operation.

Ina Wallen

I meet my husband from work and when the factory gates open and the men pour out there is only one face I look for. When I see him I feel very proud, for this man is the only person in the world who I feel safe and secure with, and I know he is looking for me with the same feelings.

Carol Akerman

Constant in a world of change, understanding in a world of indifference, loving and passionate in a world that often hates. He is the sharing of joy and sorrow, the end of loneliness, my lover and the father of my children.

Marion Marshall

A husband is the person who surrounds his woman with love, strength and security.

Lynne Patterson

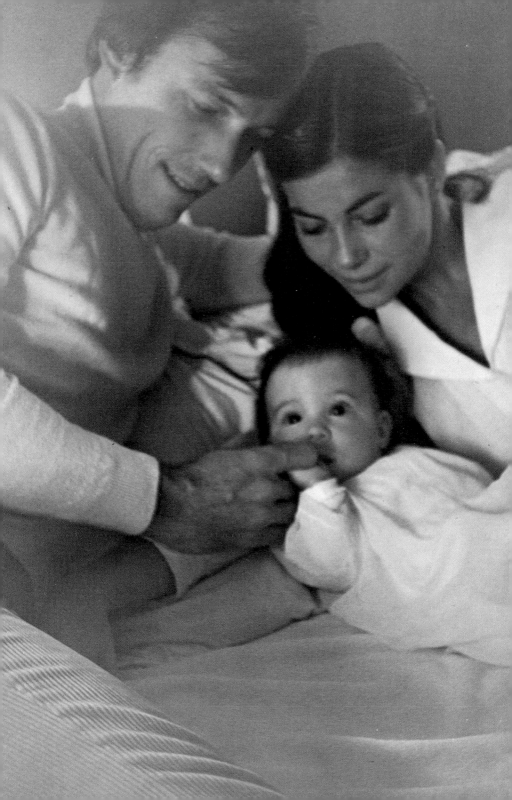

The language of love

A husband is the one whose eyes say I love you and the touch of his hand says I understand.

Hazel R Ford

He's someone who treats you like a new bride even though you've been married for years. He's the man who doesn't have to keep saying 'I love you' because you know it. It's written in his eyes for the world to see.

Linda Hall

A husband is someone whose Christmas card takes twenty times longer to choose than anyone else's because the words never mean enough.

Audrey Susan Squires

I wish I could put into words what I feel inside, not to win any competition, but so I could tell him how much I love him.

Rita Nield

He's the one who shouts and rages when I fall downstairs, but I see the fear in his eyes and know it's only because he is frightened he will lose me — that's his expression of his love.

Janine Green

A husband sends you a loving telegram, at work, and it's not even your birthday.

G Morbey

A husband is . . . so very much a part of you that you are no longer sure where his identity begins and your own identity ends — whatever his nationality, whatever yours, he speaks and understands the international language of love and you respond in the same infinite language.

Patricia de Cates

A husband is a person you're able to sit in the same room with — in silence — and not have to make polite conversation to break that silence.

Jane French

33

He is someone who sends me a bouquet of flowers and leaves me standing on the doorstep thinking . . .
It isn't my birthday. It isn't our anniversary. Not even a peace offering!
He brings tears to my eyes and complete happiness as I read the message: 'Simply because I love you'.

Suzanne Houghton

The sunshine of your life

A husband makes you wonder why you should be so lucky, when you're walking down the street in the pouring rain, laden with shopping, and you're singing to yourself — that's what a husband is!

Audrey Susan Squires

A husband is someone who lifts you up when you're down, and when you're up, stays there with you.

Tereska Barry

A husband is the sunshine through the clouds, my reason to stay sane in a world of doubtful values. He is the laughter in my eyes and the cause of any loveliness. Without his loving I am champagne that's lost it's sparkle, a life that's lost it's way.

Cathleen Deeley

He halves all my troubles and doubles all my pleasures just by being around when they happen.

Valerie Ann Hulton

Just as food without salt is tasteless, so life without my husband would be grey. He gives a meaning to life, and makes all the effort worthwhile.

Audrey P Hewitt

He's the one that makes me feel that today was a good day, but watchout — tomorrow is going to be even better.

Brenda K Goodchild

34

Back to back

Nearly two years ago, slightly scared and doubtful of the unknown future, we married. In that time my husband has become the part of me that, before, was missing. He has filled the void in me, and holds my soul.

He can make me giggle insanely, and reduce me to shrieking and crying until I'm exhausted. He can make me feel beautiful and desirable, instead of short and dumpy. He makes me glow, inside and out.

He will puzzle over the mysteries of mortgages till we both comprehend, he works many hours, quietly determined to provide my comforts. He buys me clothes, then enjoys *my* delight at *his* generosity.

He is strong physically, and in our rows he seems full of pent-up force. He can be weak and boyish, grim and serious, able to break down a locked bathroom door with a shoulder charge!

In all, a husband, *my* husband, is my other part, with whom I will fight through the joy and sadness of life, hand in hand or sometimes back to back, but always together.

Pauline Howard

Weakness in the knees

A husband is a man who, after thirty-three years of marriage, still turns my knees to water.

Mary Hughes

A quiet man, yet after nearly twenty seven years, can still, with a glance, take me to the moon.

Heather Maynard

I still go goose bumps from head to toe *every* time he kisses me.

Sandy Wallder

A husband is the warm, turning over feeling inside.

Jenifer Waters

A husband is someone who can still make your spine tingle when he unexpectedly kisses the back of your neck when you are washing up — even after seventeen years of marriage.

Jennifer Jordan

He is everything I want in one person and when we are out together I feel as young and silly as any teenager.

Valerie Rogers

The very thought of my husband is enough to bring on a smile.

Ann Martin

A husband is the man who, after you have been breathing fire and slaughter all day about the things he left undone, still makes your heart flip when he walks in unexpectedly early!

Sheila Medway

A husband is:
The ache in my heart,
The flutters in my stomach,
The jelly in my legs,
The shivers down my spine.

Sylvia Jackson

Spoiling you

A husband is someone who, seeming cheerful, ploughs his way through endless salads and cartons of cottage cheese when you're on a diet.

Helena Corless

He's the one who lectures you for spending too much money and then gives you a beautifully self-wrapped bottle of your favourite perfume.

Roberta Ben-Shushan

A husband is the man who, when we were courting, didn't hold my hand in the cinema, he held my feet because they were so cold.

Rita Hudson

A husband grumbles at the dog, then before going to bed, sneaks back in the room with an old coat to wrap around the dog because it's a cold night.

Edith Handley

A husband is someone who gets out of a warm cosy bed on a freezing cold night to crawl around on cold lino searching for a mouse that his wife is convinced is in the bedroom.

K McCurdy

A husband is someone who buys you a bottle of your favourite perfume and a beautiful card with the message, 'you always "pass" for me', when you have just failed your driving test for the third time!

Pamela Gibney

A husband is someone who sells you valuable property, when playing Monopoly with friends, to keep you in the game.

Anne Rogers

A husband puts the only hot-water-bottle in the house on your side of the bed, and wraps your nightie around it.

Margaret Davidge

A husband is the one who always saves you his last strawberry.

Kim Woodcock

He would give you the moon and stars if it was within his power.

K F Burree

A husband is someone who spends more money than he planned because of the look on your face when you saw a brown bathroom suite.

Pauline Powell

With head held high despite great embarrassment and bemused looks from neighbours he walks through a store with one large, pink, cuddly dog, purchased for you, under his arm. And that's why I'm marrying him!

Anne V Mitchell

A husband is a beautifully perceptive male who, when you're on an eternal diet, offers to bathe, towel, and ravish your sexy body, if only you won't eat that gorgeous piece of cake or pie on your plate. He replaces one temptation with another you can't refuse and further sacrifices his own waistline to eat it himself.

Linda Marshall

No doormat

A husband is a man who, because he loves you, is willing to play the fool chasing a mouse round the lounge for an evening to catch it, because you're too soft-hearted to have it killed; who will shake hands with the budgie every night because it amuses you; who will drive you mad scattering shoes, ties, jumpers and books all round the house, but whose diligence in learning to fit your dress-making is endearing; who doesn't like poetry, but writes silly poems on your Christmas presents. Yet in some subtle way he makes it clear that he's not a door-mat and you're the only person in the world he would do this for.

Gillian Ann Alford

Examples of a husband's sacrifice

He is the one who has smiled bravely through months of unemployment and given up his tobacco so that the children can still have their pocket money. Who has just left the house to go to yet another interview with hope in his heart and more faith in the future.

Valerie Young

A husband spends all his spare time under his sports car. He tightens the brakes, he rebuilds the gear box, he adjusts the carburettor, and lovingly polishes every inch of its sleek black-and-gold lines. Then he sells it to try to get a mortgage for a house.

Veronica Lockett

A husband is a man who works six days a week at a job he dislikes, and one that is a risk to his life and health, for the sake of his wife and children.

Diana Kwan

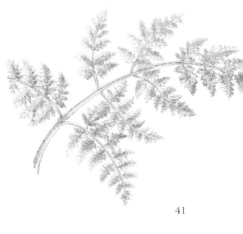

41

He's someone who turns down a chance of promotion to spend more time with his wife and daughter.

Jean Parish

A man who will convince me he doesn't want a child, because he knows I am unable to have one.

Helen Chamberlain

A husband is a man who forgives and forgets when you've been unfaithful.

Harriet Drummond

He is the saint who cared for *your* aged parents as if they were his own.

Mary Horton

A husband is the person who'll do anything for you — even let you go.

Frances Thomas

A family again

A husband doesn't have to be the man you walked down the aisle with and fathered your children. A husband can be the man who first saw you lonely and sad, struggling hard to bring up your two small children alone. He can be the man who, when you were depressed and low, told you how courageous you were; who, when you doubted your own ability, told you you were a natural mother – a thoughtful friend to your children.

When you are sitting in a pub with a very attractive friend who's surrounded by boyfriends, your man tells you he loves your charming quiet voice and smile, and convinces you that too much glamour attracts the wrong kind of guy.

He can come into your life and bring smiles and laughter to your children. He can help build your house into a home. He can take three cockney sparrows into the countryside and teach them the names of trees and insects and flowers, to open up a whole new world to you where you tread grass, ride ponies and fish in lakes.

He switches off your television and reads to you, discusses things that at one time you thought you weren't capable of understanding. He can promise to build you a new bathroom and when it's half done, he sees the sun shining and makes you rush out with him to the nearest park where he plays silly games and you feel like a kid again, chasing you, fighting you, making you tumble to the ground and forgetting any worries you had, you laugh and giggle and love him.

He can infuriate you because he's late for everything, forgetful, and because he never finishes your bathroom, or anything he ever starts.

He can lay beside you in your bed – and transform you from laughing playmate into lover.

He can be the man you wake up to in the morning and, seeing him lying there, you know life's worth living again.

He's the man that made you a family.

C Quinn

He can come into your life and bring smiles and laughter to your children.

C Quinn

The second time around

A husband is someone who loves you with no questions asked when you have been married before, and got two children. He is the one who helps you through guilt stricken nights and black days of remorse, never wishing he could go back and be on his own. He is a good 'father' to another man's family. Most of all he is someone, who, in the last two years has given his heart and soul to me, and in doing so restored to me self respect, and the ability to see that one mistake need not colour the rest of my life. In fact he is my best friend.

A Davis

Well, life with my first husband was rather like living in a concentration camp. Complete with torture chamber. Thought maybe I was paying off sins incurred in a previous existence. Then came a very bleak period. Divorce. Financial and housing hassles. Worry over work. The loneliness of the one-parent family.
And now, with my second husband? It's like coming out of a deep, dark, cold cave into the sunlight. Letting your hair stream in the wind, listening to laughter. It's snuggling up together, sharing the joy, the fun, the tears, the work. It's having time to be yourself. It's never letting the sun set on a tiff, and just simply being there when needed. A husband is your whole reason why.

Margaret Dobson

A husband, to me, is one who comes along when you've been a widow for twenty years, working too hard, relaxing too little. He comes along and despite the fact that you're overweight makes you feel like Miss World.
He provides you with fresh vegetables from the garden and roses — planted so that you can see them from the kitchen window. I have never won anything in my life, but somehow I got the most wonderful prize.

Enid Zinn

At fifty-one, and two years a widow, happiness returned to my life — I am once again loved and honoured.

B I Fordyce

A husband is the man who can re-awaken feeling locked away, I thought for ever.

After discovering tragically that my first husband had married me bigamously I died a little inside. I was left with a newborn baby and no means of support. I was one of the lucky ones, I had a devoted mum who made sacrifices to allow me to take up nursing studies. I completed my training and am now going on to better things. That is all in the past and two years ago I met Robert , a quiet but fun-loving guy.

...the man who made me laugh again.

...the man who makes me hopeful again of a life worth living.

...the man who made me remember that fun and laughter is part of my right as a person.

M Philips

For better — and worse

What is a husband? Well for my money I would bet on the man I married in September of last year. I met him through a lonely hearts ad. after spending six years on my own, divorced, bringing up four children. After a struggle we managed to survive with me taking two jobs to make ends meet. But the problems were endless, one teenager leaving home, another having a near fatal car accident, having two fires in the house, an electric meter robbed, an oil tank bursting after just being filled and various other problems. You can imagine I needed a shoulder to lean on. I put an advertisement in the local paper and the answer to my prayers arrived at fifty two. He was widowed and an airline pilot. I met him in February and by September we had both sold our houses and bought a larger modern house big enough for the six of us.

You ask what is a husband, well I'll tell you. It's someone who loves you so much he accepts all your faults, your tempers, your irritable ways. Comforts you when you are tired. Cleans, cooks and shops for you when you are working full time. Takes you in his arms and loves you when you think you can't see a way out of a problem with your children.

Someone who helps buy a motor bike for a son when he has a job miles away and when he breaks down my husband fetches him and rushes around for spare parts and helps repair it. Someone who takes your daughter for interviews and collects her reports from school and watches her swimming for her school and disciplines and corrects them, but loves them all the same because they belong to me. Gives money for discos and collects them at night. And, when your nerves are bad and you think he'll walk out because he must have had enough, stays because he loves you, (even when you look awful after having your hair cut and dyed back brown, when he loved it blond and long.)

That's what I call a husband and I think he's wonderful and I adore him and I only hope I can make him as happy as he's made me.

Iris Ann Forman

Loving your children

A husband is a man who takes on four horrors and loves them as his own, when he really loves his solitude.

E Simons

A husband is someone like mine, a man who has taken on another man's child as his own. He collects my son from school during his afternoon tea-break then takes him back to work, so that he won't be in the house alone, because I go to work also.

Barbara Gavin

I think I'm lucky to have such a husband. He spent our wedding night in our bed cuddling my three-year-old son who was ill with a fever and sickness.

Lynn Court

A husband is the guy who picks you up and dusts you down. Then he marries you and looks after your son and he tells the little chap, 'You were the best so I picked you and they threw Mummy in too'.

G Guy

Chauvinists anonymous

He's someone who believes that the fairies come in and do the cooking, cleaning, and washing.

He's never even *heard* of Women's Lib, or if he has he totally ignores it.
A husband admires strange blondes in low cut dresses, but you must stay mousey and wear your old dress – it's cheaper.

A husband moans because the house is a mess, and then blames you for tidying up his spirit level.

He treats you like a queen one day and a part of the furniture the next.

When my husband retired he promised to help with the chores so that we could have days out together. However, within a month or two we had acquired a continental quilt to help with the bedmaking and a tea-maker so there is no argument as to who gets the tea in the morning.
I was to do the cooking and he the washing up. Guess what? We now have a dishwasher.

A husband is someone who has his own restaurant, automatic tea machine and launderette.

He is annoyed when his favourite shirt isn't ready to wear, then asks, 'Why don't you sit down and relax more often?'

A husband is someone who after he has eaten a good evening meal, and has just realized you aren't feeling well says, 'Never mind dear, you get washed up and we will have an early night'.

A husband likes to imagine he is the brains of the marriage. He gives detailed accounts on how to economise on the weekly shopping bill by purchasing items marked '1p off' and then proceeds to feed the one armed bandit in the local with 10p after 10p!

He's the man who ought to be a millionaire if it depended upon how hard you work.

48

He sometimes moans if I have a whim for new clothes. Then he'll give me the money after he's done his 'mans' master bit.

He's someone who in days gone by
Had eyes for only me,
But now he looks at others,
In the daily 'Sun' – page three.

A husband is a person that:- expects you to *know* all that he does not know, expects you to *do* all that he does not do. Yet still tells you, you have no brains, no sense, no taste, no nothing.

He is the person who is allowed to drop his cigarette ash on the kitchen floor. He is the one who does not need to wear a safety belt and can smoke as often as he wants – after all, he's always right, isn't he?!

A husband is two feet sticking out from under a car every week-end.

A husband expects his tea lying ready for him when he comes home. Then he goes to the boozer.

A husband is a go-getter . . .
It's go get this,
and go get that.

A husband is the person
who does not know where
the cups are kept after
twenty-two years of
marriage.

Liberated ladies

He is the individual who gives you enough rope to allow independence yet, in doing so, holds you to him in strong bonds of love.

Lesley Cox

He is arrogant and a worthy adversary with whom to spar in defence of my equality as a woman.

Phyllis Anderson

If I leave the cleaning and dusting so that I can write a book he thinks it is fun, and writes 'I love you' in the dust on the dressing table.

J C Bailey

According to the taxman and the Passport Office, he's practically my owner. According to my mother, his mother and most people over fifty, he's my lord and master. According to the bank manager, the Building Society, the Electricity Board and travelling salesmen, he's the head of the household. And according to us? Well, he's just half of us.

Gwenno Hywyn

Unliberated ladies?

A husband is a woman's true liberator.
He will free her from that most suffocating of prisons, self-consideration.
She has only to abandon such words as 'exploitation', 'equality' and 'rights', and wallow unashamedly in 'consideration', 'love' and 'encouragement', and freedom can be hers.
A happy marriage is the nearest most of us get to a state of grace on this earth. Why not join us 'liberated' women and find out for yourself!

J R Little

A husband makes you enjoy being one of the domestic morons you always detested.

S J Colby

If you forget your role as wife don't expect your husband to be a husband.

Christine Kouzoupis

A husband is someone who treats you like his slave but makes you feel like a queen.

Mary Jensen

If marriage is bondage I never want to be free.

Jean Rupert

How can women want to be equal? And join the women's lib when there is such a wonderful being as a husband?

Jean Tainton

Naggers anonymous

My husband is so lazy about the house and doesn't do a thing to help. I've learnt to decorate myself: in the midst of it, he'll shout from his fireside chair (watching TV) 'How about a cup of tea!' Dirty washing's left where it comes off, on the bedroom floor, drawers left open — I could go on and on.

He's a man who buys a huge greyhound and leaves you to take it for walks. He's also someone who leaves clothes lying on the floor, doesn't wipe his muddy boots at the door, seems to always knock ashtrays over, and leave empty milk cartons in the fridge.

A husband gets egg on his chin, leaves muddy footprints in the hall, and throws his socks under the bed.

He never makes the bed, puts the top on the toothpaste, nor puts his clothes away properly.

He is the most aggravating, infuriating man I have ever met, especially when he forgets to put the lid back down on the loo!

A husband is someone who squeezes the toothpaste from the middle and always leaves the top off.

etc etc etc

An endangered species

A husband is a physically attractive breadwinning, beerswilling specimen of the genus MAN, with strong sexual drive and latent paternal instincts.
Becoming rare over the last decade he, nevertheless, is a delight to observe in his native semi-detached habitat where he displays his inimitable nest-feathering and brood-rearing qualities.
Mere wife though I am, I can but marvel at the sheer superiority of this endangered species and know there are many of you who would like to capture a specimen of your own.
A word of caution. This breed can never be completely tamed and should not be caged — an illusion of freedom being necessary. Although difficult to house-train, they respond to kindness and can become affectionate pets.

Kitt Hicks

A big softy

He's the typical 'no-nonsense', mustn't show his feelings, English boy, who wept when you refused his first proposal of marriage.

Jenny Clements

He is a tough as they come in business and yet he can be moved to tears by the death of one of the children's pets or when I relate to him some small progress our young handicapped niece has made.

Maureen Shillam

A husband is a man who doesn't grumble when I nearly burn down our flat. But nearly faints when I cut my finger carving the meat.

Angela Cook

A husband dreads to see me ill because he begins to feel ill too.

Sarah Hirschfield

A husband is secretly soft over babies and rabbits.

Clare Ryder

*A husband is the tough 'hombre'
with the marshmallow centre.*

Joan M Best

A man for all moods

A sense of humour is a must in any husband. With us women they need it.

Lynn Christine Webb

A husband is a big gentle, soft-footed man who is always ready to act as unpaid psychoanalyst for hours.

Marianna Kostis

He is the one who sits patiently holding his hands in front of him pretending to be a pelvis whilst you endlessly practise delivering a breech teddy-bear!

Susan Shufflebottom

A husband is a person who swallows lumpy custard smiling and bravely asks for more. Who struggles into his favourite sweater after you shrunk it in the wash and says he prefers a closer fit.

Carol McGarrity

He lets me warm my cold hands on his back or tummy and will play 'I spy' with me when I can't sleep.

Teresa Morley

A husband is someone who puts up with the times you haven't washed your hair, or have a nasty tummy bug, or are being too nasty for words ... for a lifetime.

Linda Cornish

A husband is someone to moan at when I feel like moaning.

Sophia King

A husband is someone who can take the sting out of a pre-menstrual hang up by being nice and saying, 'You know, when you're cross your eyes go a beautiful deep shade of sea green'.

Denise Scot Goodwin

He is someone who can smile and hug me without a word, after I've been a right bitch.

Helen Morgan

A husband is someone who will listen patiently while you call him the most selfish being in the world, and then leave the room — only to return with a cup of tea.

Kathleen M Bowman

When the cat's been sick on the new hall carpet, and the kids have brought you a dead bumble bee to resuscitate, and that new recipe with all the cream has stuck to the saucepan, and you round on him and shriek, 'It's all your fault — I hate you' and know for sure that he still loves you — that's a husband.

Carol Bunn

A husband is a man for all moods.

Hilary Thornton

You sexy thing!

A husband is the lover who never has to go home.

Hilary Marchant

A husband should be able to charm the hind leg off a donkey, think young, and last of all he had better be a damn good lover.

Jane Sarah Wilkins

A husband is someone who buys you a sexy nightdress and makes certain you never wear it out sleeping in it.

Peggy Mais

A husband makes one feel desirable. He pours champagne over his wife when she is emerging from the bath and then proceeds to drink it off.

Susan Perkins

A husband is somone who pretends he's a Viking and tears your only nightie off your back in the middle of winter because 'Vikings don't take no for an answer'.

Genevieve Cotrell

He's super, sixty and sexy.

J Viner

He is a lover who makes love to me without seeming to notice I am two stone overweight, and makes me feel like a film star.

Margaret Knowles

I know sex is not supposed to be the most important thing in marriage but to me it is the crowning beauty of a beautiful marriage. To be so close, to share such heights, to breathe such joy together is something I never dreamed of. It renews us week after week, year after year.

Helen M Thomson

A gentle husband can turn a shy plain girl like me into a wow of a mistress.

Brenda Johnson

A husband ignores your new sexy nightie . . . then attacks you in the broom cupboard when the cabbage is boiling over.

Denise Hawthorne

Mr. Lazybones

A husband is someone who says yes to what you want him to do, but is still sitting there when you've done it.

Deborah Collins

A husband runs a mile at the sight of a lawn mower.

Cynthia Smith

A husband is someone who *means* to repair things.

B Pearce

Thank you for working so hard to give us a nice home although I would still like some shelves in the living room. You promised them a couple of years ago.

F Kingsley

A husband is someone who is very just — just going to do this, just going to do that, just when you want a job done.

S Walker

A husband is a person who promises to Hoover — later — do the dishes — later — cut the grass — later!

Daphne James

If there is a nail that needs hammering in anywhere round the house, why is it I have to do it when he is a carpenter?

Elaine Chalmers

My husband is a bundle of aggravations tied with strings of half-finished, forgotten-about, man-about-the-house jobs.

L Harvey

A husband is someone who says 'I'll cook dinner' and buys fish and chips.

Elizabeth Williams

A husband is too tired to fix that leaking tap but makes it to the pub.

Judith Lett

A husband has a dutiful ear but grunts in all the wrong places.

Vivienne Fox

He provides honourable excuses for doing nothing when household mechanisms are doing likewise.

J S Barber

A husband is someone who says 'I'll do the dishes', and manages to walk into the kitchen just as the last dish has been wiped.

Susan Edwards

Before he was discharged from the Royal Navy he told me that I would never require a window cleaner again but of course you can't clean them when the sun is shining on them nor when it is cloudy.

Geraldine Fitzgerald

A husband is someone who asks if you would like another cup of tea or another slice of toast, on hearing you say, 'yes, please', says, 'while you're up get me one too'.

Brenda Adams

Frank Spencers

My husband is a 'Frank Spencer' about the house (DISASTER!!). He sometimes goes deaf when being spoken to, doesn't like to change his socks and *will not* peel spuds.
Overall he's my ideal — cuddly and considerate, loving, jolly and my best pal! I'd never swap him — but any offers??

Pam Mabey

A husband is someone who, whilst putting up cupboards, drops the hammer and makes a hole in the draining board.

Betty Gardner

A husband is my handyman who will take three days mending a leak under the sink, spend a small fortune buying new washers, seatings, then taps and a blowlamp, to save wasting money on a plumber; meanwhile forcing the family into a hasty retreat from his rage and vocabulary — finally admitting defeat when every available saucepan is overflowing and calls in a plumber who has the job done in minutes and charges a minimal fee!

A Jacobs

My husband is the only person I know who wears two odd socks every time he changes them, puts pictures up that fall down two days later, regularly gets covered in mud while attempting to garden, and takes his eyes out every night to polish!

Anne McCleod

He is a man who drills seven holes in the kitchen wall to fix one can-opener. He isn't tall, dark or handsome, but *hands off, he's mine!*

Sharon M Scott

Helpless and hopeless!

A husband is cigar smoke surrounding an armchair giving his theory on coping with home and the family scene. Theory which was devastated with one small attempt at practice, which resulted in a burnt out frying pan and only the *handle* of the slicer.

Suzanne Murray

He thinks it nothing to have a baby. 'Women in India have them by the side of the road', he remarks casually. But one little sneeze and he takes to his bed with all the cold remedies. Husbands, bless them, are here to stay.

Sarah Jones

A husband is someone who brings his sick wife a tray with a boiled egg, toast, salt, orange juice and a red rose and says 'Darling, where do you keep my clean socks?'.

J M Schofield

A husband is the enigma who copes admirably with the intricacies of income tax and insurance but who can never find his comb or his tie.

Catherine Hamilton

A husband is the man who does one job and makes six for you.

Helen Douch

A husband is the one that finds when we arrive at our honeymoon hotel, he had packed a tie for every day of the week and nothing else.

Heather Rooks

A husband is the one who makes the bed and leaves the sheets off.

Patricia Murray

Quarrels and making up

A husband is someone you love for hours and can only hate for minutes.

Janet Melless

A husband is a sparring partner (sometimes leaving for ever, only to be back the same evening).

Fay Salmon

A small argument with him can worry you more than a third world war.

June McDermott

I wouldn't change him for anything even though he won't have a blustering good row.

Wendy Doreen Hanson

He's the one who makes you laugh when you're trying so hard to be cross.

Nancy Buchanan

He's the one who you will purposely start an argument with, because the kiss and make-up is so worthwhile.

Michele Monro

A husband is someone who buys me chocolates when we quarrel, then eats them himself.

Laura Sender

A husband is the one who wins most of the arguments only to pretend he gave in gracefully.

Cheryl Forward

A husband is a person who always likes to have the last word but doesn't always succeed.

Carol Redman

He shouts, I shout. He storms out of the front door, then he sneaks in the back door, heartily slaps my bum, then tickles me till I am helpless.

Janine Green

A husband is a man with whom to <u>share</u> a quarrel with no hard feelings afterwards.

Edith Handley

A husband can so infuriate you that you could commit murder. His.

R S Harris

He's someone who never seems to lose his temper, which really infuriates me!

Sheelagh E Taylor

The only reason you throw the suitcase at him is because you know he won't pack it.

E Leaver

A husband never does make the tea, coffee, or anything else because he says 'you do it better' and who after driving you mad will turn his soulful eyes and amazed expression on you and say 'Darling you must not yell like that.'

J Rainbow

A husband is the only person who can shout and bellow at you and get away with it without apologising.

Catherine Hunter

A husband is happiness after an argument.

Denise Pritchard

Peculiar habits

A husband is someone who stands around in his shirt and socks and wonders what you are laughing at.

Cindy Harvey

A husband gets up at 3 to practise his Morris dancing.

Mary Bonnett

My husband does Kermit the Frog impressions when I'm depressed.

Pennie Howard

He is someone who clicks his toes in the middle of your favourite TV programme.

Karen Calvert

A husband is a man who leaves his dirty socks under the bed, who walks into the house in muddy gumboots when you have just done all the cleaning, who puts his maggots (for fishing) in the fridge.

Lise Smart

A husband is someone who, while curled up in front of the 'box' with a coffee at his side and the inevitable choccie bikkie at the ready, will suddenly pull off both his socks and proceed to pick his toenails and place the discarded items in a meticulous little pile on the arm of his chair, beside the choccie bikkie.

Margaret James

Mine is a button twiddler.

Irene M Wild

Only a husband would start to knock a hole in the upstairs ceiling for a trap door ten minutes before Sunday lunch.

J Welton

When bored he takes the lid off the flush cistern and tries to improve the plumbing. His kink is shoe cleaning, without fail, every evening at 10pm.

Ruth Wilson

*The trouble is
you only find out
the horrifying truths
after you marry them.*

Barbara Simmonds

A husband is someone who dances frenziedly like Max Wall round the kitchen telling jokes at the same time even though you are collapsing from stomach-cramping hysterics, someone who has to take apart — 'just to see how it works' — the iron, the radio, the electric radiators, the rented television — YIKES!

Someone who sings at the top of his voice when driving any distance over about three miles, and pulls faces at himself in the bathroom mirror; who dutifully wears those hand-knitted jumpers which would look more appropriate on a person a foot shorter and two feet broader! Someone who plays the guitar in every spare second at home, who likes froth in his bath and hates nylon sheets and greens.

If this sounds unlike any husband you know, that's because he's mine and he's unique.

Mary B Mitchell

Coming down with a bump

A husband is the one who says life will be a bed of roses, forgetting to mention *you* will have to weed it.

Jill Hague

A husband is someone who leads you up the aisle then drives you round the bend!

M Bolton

A husband is someone who buys flowers in the first year, and then presents you with shears and a mower the next year.

J Ayris

He's the one who offered me life on a farm, then handed me the muck fork.

Jill Hague

A husband is somebody who loved you best in your mini *before*, but nearly fainted when you wore it *after*!

Linda Shand

A husband is a Sir Galahad who rescues you from a fate worse than death (being left on the shelf at twenty-four) and takes you away on his charger, (a beaten up Ford) and then deposits you at a kitchen sink full of dishes.

M Shelbourne

A husband used to buy flowers and chocolates, now he brings pork chops and sausages.

Jean Tabrah

Unromantic thing

After a quarrel he brings a bunch of daffs so tightly wrapped in newspaper that you think it's a pound of rhubarb.

Ruth Yvonne Heap

The lights are low, there's music on,
The setting is romantic, I'm waiting for John.
Something special for his tea,
I hope he'll like it; we'll wait and see.
In he comes, looks around,
Up go the lights, off goes the 'sound'.
'Well', he started bleating,
'I like to see what I'm eating'.
By now he's put the TV on,
Could it be romance has gone?

Elizabeth Shearer

He takes your hand when they play your tune, but attributes the wrong occasion and significance to it.

E D Dowd

He never brings red roses to say he loves me
But he does bring the odd red cabbage.
Could it really be for me,
Or do you think it's for his tea?

Dorothy May Mason

A husband tells you that buying Valentine cards is only another nasty scheme by the taxman to take taxpayer's money off him.

Jennifer Pirie

A husband is a former romantic lover, who now prefers to enjoy a 'dirty week-end' shovelling smelly compost in the garden looking like some scarecrow in wellies. But if he brings you a cabbage, 'tis but a rose by any other name.'

Anne Sims

65

Comfortable, like old slippers

What is a husband?
Well, you know what an old slipper is like? Comforting. Oh, so comforting. I guess he's an old slipper!

Brenda Walker

Any woman who is happily married knows that there are no words to describe a husband, he is just a very 'comfy' feeling deep inside your heart.

S Skinner

A husband is like a favourite and well-loved armchair; always in the way when you do the housework; outer covering in constant need of repair; sitting smugly in the corner of the living room while you juggle with saucepans in the kitchen; harbouring the cat when she should be outside in the garden; jumped on and attacked by favourite nieces, nephews and dogs; silently listening to your jumbled description of the days events; but always there at the end of the day, like an old friend, with a welcoming look, for you to curl up on, be comfortable with, and the best place in the world for you to fall asleep.

Priscilla A Baily

Just a potato

A husband is like a potato – eyes everywhere (when girls are about) fatally attracted to mud (on football pitches), worms (for fishing) and requires frequent watering (at the local). Like the sturdy potato a husband is satisfying, hard to give up and a good solid friend throughout life. He may not be much to look at and perhaps is sometimes dull, but can soon be revitalised by a loving wife. And when you smile especially for him that hard exterior can turn into mash in minutes.

Margaret Dobson

A husband is like an old pair of boots. Worn but warm and reliable.

Patricia Clift

Sad stories

I know that I shall never be married now. I am middle-aged and ever since I was four years of age I have been lame, due to a T.B. hip.

My dream would be to have a kind, loving husband. A strong arm to lean on in times of trouble, and also just someone to talk over the little ordinary things of day-to-day living. A bulwark against some of the cruelties of the outside world. To be a couple instead of always alone, the odd one out.

Someone to cook and clean for, never mind women's lib, that indeed would be enough for me.

Loneliness is indeed one of the worst afflictions for people like me.

Patricia Jones

A husband is someone who comes home at night and puts an arm around you, someone to comfort you in grief, and to tell you once in a while he loves you — just three little words but those words mean everything.

For you see, I have never had any of these things.

I have had fourteen pregnancies, and only five left. My daughter died three years ago quite suddenly at 16, one age 4 years and the rest as babies. In my grief all I got was, 'They're dead now, there's nothing I can do about it or bring them back'.

If I asked him if he enjoyed his meal the answer would be, 'That's your job, a woman's place is in the home'.

My husband died eighteen months ago and I still never know whether or not he loved me, but I can still have my dreams and thoughts of what I would have liked in a husband.

Linda Gardner

A husband is someone to share your highest hopes and dreams, and joy in the family, and to come home in the evening from work and settle to a lovely comfortable night together. I had all these things for almost thirty seven years. My dreams crashed six months ago when I learned my husband was visiting another woman and also going to bed with her. He flatly denies this, but I've watched him come and go, and with a breaking heart, I've turned for refuge in my home. I watch and wait, and pray and hope that one day he will come home again in the way we used to know.

I would appeal to these women who take other women's husbands, to think of the anguish, heartbreak and pain a wife goes through. I sit down and try to think — why — has this happened to us.

How I envy you happy couples. Bless them all.

Clare Usher

When my husband repeated our wedding vows twenty years ago I little realised how much he would have to stand by them. Ours was a happy courtship, and we had five happy years before I conceived for our first baby and sadly our only to be child. Everything was ready in the nursery and we were longing for our baby. Labour was to last three days and the final stage three hours. All the pain was forgotten when I held my baby, darling Susan, in my arms.

The happiness was not to last. Depression was to hit me. I was sent to a nearby mental hospital. My husband's life was shattered. It took almost a year before I was really well. My husband helped me to gain my confidence and to take no notice of the whispers. We put it all behind us and we were truly happy. Out of the blue I had a relapse and these were to continue for fourteen years. I could write a book on my experiences in a mental hospital and how I have seen mental health improve. They told me I was lucky to have a husband to stand by me, most men leave their wives when the strain and stress becomes too much.

The final toll was yet to come, my doctor was surprised to find me pregnant. They wouldn't let me go through with it. I was to have an abortion. Three days after the sad operation I was ill again back in hospital. I was to put Norman and all my family through hell. My husband stood by me, finally not knowing what he was doing or saying.

Slowly I got better. There is a happy ending we hope to this story. I have been told a new drug will keep me free from attacks. My husband has surely stood the real test of marriage.

He is so kind and patient and loving. I love him so.

Jean Wright Hopper

A husband is someone who falls in love with you on sight and changes from being a near alcoholic, trying to kill himself through drink, to a sober, tender father of two beautiful daughters. Not easy.

Only to find out two years later that he is dying of scirosis of the liver, a ruptured stomach and blood pressure.

Someone who instead of 'hitting the bottle' again, at this news, simply does everything in his power to make sure his wife and children will be provided for, even though it means he has to do

69

without most luxuries when he's alive and is probably shortening his life more with overwork. Someone who never mentions his illness again but who you occasionally catch crying at the thought of his daughters becoming teenagers without his guidance. He's a man who's only ambition for himself is to be loved.

Emily Wilkinson

There is an emptiness here in our home,
The reliable fixture I thought I had,
That special person the kids called Dad,
Someone you don't value till you're alone,
Just a visitor now and again,
Friends now not lovers, it's not the same,
What is a husband? you ask,
A memory past.
In my heart he will lay,
That at least can't go away.

Louise Wallace

A husband is someone who dominates you. He takes you — body and soul — as his property, to do his will. Then, during a row, when you try to fight back a little and he tells you he is leaving; he is the one you beg to stay with you — because without him *life is nothing*.

Angela Solomon

For me a husband would be someone who would listen to me reciting 'To a Mouse' by Rabbie Burns. Give me a bathroom with soft white carpets. Take me to the sea in the rain and bring me forget-me-knots. See me in the blue see-through nightie I've never worn. Tell me stretch marks are beautiful.
And a husband would be the father my little son has never had.

Jane Kent

Until death us do part

When you lose your husband the bottom drops out of your world and you are without the best friend and lover you ever could wish for, the person who motivates your every thought. When you don't have him any more, you have time to remember all the little things.

C Allen

A husband, I thought, was an irritating, boring, thoughtless, bad-tempered, unnecessary appendage. Now I think he was a very unhappy man, trying desperately hard to make our marriage happy and never quite succeeding, and after thirty years of marriage I didn't recognise his qualities.

Why do I feel differently now? He died last December and I miss him, whatever he was.

Patricia Kennedy

A husband is someone whose after-shave you still keep around because it reminds you.

J M Morrison

When gone, he is the reason you wonder what it was all about — the reason you sometimes feel guilty and often bewildered. He is the other half of your life — without which you feel nothing — and even less when stark reality is a narrow buff-backed allowance book and a new very low tax code number from the Welfare State.

Margaret Simmons

A husband, to a widow like me, is a memory of 'a vanished hand and the sound of a voice that is still'. Those words are on my husband's tombstone.

Look after him while you have him, you wives. Remember he's only mortal.

H Bailey

A husband is a whole world of company that you only know you had after you have lost him.

Jo Logan

When he is gone there seems nothing, just an emptiness.

Audrey Nelsey

He is someone you are so comfortable with, you take for granted and think he will always be there to lean on, until suddenly you are left with memories of togetherness and a void that even your wonderful children cannot fill.

Here's to all husbands.

Vera Walmsley

A husband is a man who looks at you and says 'that's the girl for me'. A man whose qualities are revealed by the way he stands by you, who shows through the ages how much you mean. Whose going leaves a blank, a feeling of 'lost' in a world in which you have never before been alone. He doesn't have to be a this or a that, just that particular kind of man you took the 'highs' and the 'lows' with. And when you've picked up the threads of your life, you say to yourself, if you never do another thing in your life but enjoy what there is left to enjoy, you've lived life to the full. For he was that kind of man.

S Foster

In sickness . . .

He brought me home from hospital looking like something out of Belsen, after several operations for cancer. The first time he lifted me in and out of the bath and I saw myself in the mirror I went hysterical with the shock, and he knelt down and kissed all over the repulsive looking scars, thanking God that he hadn't lost me.

Mary Scotland

In my opinion a husband is a man who says breast cancer is just a different outlook on life and that a masectomy just means the same beautiful lady, just a little lopsided.

Mary Allison

When we married two and a half years ago, I was a pretty, bubbly, happy go lucky wife. Then after only three months of marriage, I developed anorexia nervosa. I became depressed, bad tempered, and obviously did not look anything like the girl he married. He watched me go through months of hospital treatment that failed. He put up with nasty taunting remarks from his work mates. Through two years of this, however, he has very rarely lost his temper and has never lost his cheerful optimism. Now I feel that my gradual recovery is entirely due to my husband's unflagging encouragement and his down to earth approach to the problems we have had.

Jenny McBride

A husband is someone to love unconditionally. If you trust your heart, there are no regrets.
He has seen me through two major heart operations, the last one in 1976, when I lost my speech and my right arm was paralysed. But in the distance, when I seemed to be in 'limbo', he kissed me and said 'I love you' so many times a day and I knew then I had to get well because the bond of our love was passing from him to me .

Betty Carruthers

A husband is someone who marries you for better or for worse. Who comes home from a hard day's manual work and overtime, and has to do the housework and sometimes has to cook his own meals and who never moans about it. Who, when I am down and depressed, and think I would be better off out of it all, says 'I would rather have you ill but with me than not here at all', and I love him dearly for it. You see, he is having the 'for worse' part because I have multiple sclerosis.

Mary Angela Farish

When he's away

Alone in a crowd I can feel isolated in secret joy just thinking of him.

N Payne

He is only as far from me, as thoughts are from thinking.

Linda Elizabeth Hope

A husband can make me cry into the phone by just the tone of his voice telling me that he's missing me.

C P French

A husband is someone who is there all the time, even when he is far away.
He is the scent of aftershave, the shelves upon the wall, the papers lying around, the spring bulbs in the garden, the pipe ash in every ash tray. He is the wallpaper on the walls, the fitted furniture in the bedroom, the tiles in the bathroom, the units in the kitchen, the dirty socks on the bedroom floor.
Who is my husband? He is me. I am him. He is the man I love. He is the man who loves me.

Christine H Seed

My husband is someone who travels seventy-six miles by sea in gale force winds every weekend for the six years we've been married to spend a day with us, who walks half a mile through dockland in order to use a telephone that isn't broken just to talk to me for three minutes, who writes me a love letter every week, who buys me chocs even though I'm on a diet, who brought me back to life when I thought life was over for me, who became daddy to my three little children when their daddy was taken tragically from them, who tells me to economise after he's read the letter from the bank manager, then pays £1.20 for flowers, who's sexy and gorgeous, and who I love.

V Jennings

When he's not there he leaves 'holes', but a warmth to fill them and confidence to enjoy moments alone.

Valerie May

74

Growing old together

Last Christmas when he gave me a new wedding ring he said he would marry me all over again (and so would I). Nothing else needs to be said after nineteen years of marriage.

P Hardy

I really should know what a husband is. I was courted by him for four years from the age of fifteen years, and have now been married for fifty-three years. We have produced two very nice considerate children and now have fourteen grandchildren and one great grandchild. We had a wonderful golden wedding party organised by the children. My son gave us some money for a holiday so my husband took me a few hundred miles across the sea to Cologne, Germany, and took me on the same street corner, where so many years ago (1920) as a British Tommy, he gave me my first kiss. He kissed me there again on exactly the same spot. I apologize to having repeated the word WE so many times, but with such a wonderful man it had to be WE.

Trudy Neale

A husband is someone who probably has more faults than virtues. You recognise the faults only one at a time, and forgive them just as quickly – but the virtues, as you discover each one, add up to something you cherish.

Catherine Barry

A husband is a warm cosy glow that steals over you when you hear his key in the door, and a dear liar to boot when he tells you that you still look as lovely as you did thirty-five years ago.

Lavinia Martin

He continues to 'woo' his wife into old age, realising that they are both still individuals, ever-changing, with private thoughts, private feelings, and private silences.

Joan Donaldson

A good husband is the greatest blessing. You wake up each morning thanking God that you have another day together.

M Killoran

A husband is the person on whose arm you once 'floated' up the aisle. This, then, seemed the culmination of all your dreams — it was actually only the beginning.

Very soon a husband has become the person to whom you can feel free to express any opinions, personal doubts. The person who is exciting, untidy, exasperating, encouraging, lovable and always there, slowly becoming a part of you.

Then the husband is also the father; taking second place, worrying with you over decisions being made on behalf of another life — medical, educational and moral.

The passage of time brings the situation to one of advice being sought but apparently disregarded. However, you grasp the opportunities of more time together again. More time being spent with the person you are no longer 'in love' with but realize you love still.

Suddenly the realization that the husband has become the favourite companion of a grandson as well as the steadying hand now that you are no longer so sure on your feet. He's that slow shuffle you recognise as he brings the bedtime drinks — the person who has shared your hopes, dreams, mistakes and your stake in the future. A husband has become the reflection of your life.

Margaret Fraser

He's the sweet permanence left to his wife when the telegrams are yellow with age and the icing has long since crumbled away on that preserved piece of wedding cake.

Margot Hargreaves

A husband never feels too old to hold hands.

S Manuelpillai

As the years go by you get closer and learn to give and take. Children add a bonus, then the grandchildren, another lovely sharing, and your love is more precious.

B Keeble

A husband, like all the best things in life, grows more and more precious the longer you have him.

J L Hanson

My husband?
It's hard to explain,
He is the boy I danced with — to *Charmaine*.
Yet he is 'Grandad', playing the clown,
My backer upper, my calmer down.
He's a young father, a broad shoulder,
A good pal, now we are older.
He is sanity, he's laughter,
He's 'happy ever after'.
A grey thatch
A bald patch,
But then again —
He's the boy I danced with, to *Charmaine*.

D M Walker

A husband is the one you hope to die before — so that you are
never left without him.

M Larter

My husband is someone I love so much that a lifetime is not long
enough to share with him.

M Johns

Is there a birthday coming up soon?

If you enjoyed *What is a Husband?* why not order another of these gift books? They make lovely presents for special occasions, birthdays, Mother's Day, and Christmas.

To Mum, £1.95
'If I threw a rock at my mother she'd still love me.'
A thoughtful, joyful gift.

To Dad, £1.95
'Fathers are always right, and even if they're not right, they're never actually wrong.'

Grandmas & Grandpas, £1.95
'A grandma is old on the outside and young on the inside.'

Happy Families £1.95
"A family is a mother and father to love, and a brother or sister to fight with." A lovely gift for any member of the family.

Shopping by Post, £4.50 (£1.95 paperback)
Whether you want a needle-threader or a folding bicycle by post, this book tells you which firm to write to.

See Britain at Work, £4.95
The first guidebook of its kind. 300 glassworks, potteries, power stations, car plants and small craft industries you can visit.

Order any of these books through your bookshop — or send a cheque or postal order to Exley Publications, 63 Kingsfield Road, Watford WD1 4PP.